BRITAIN IN OLD PHOTOGRAPHS

# WALTON-ON-THAMES & WEYBRIDGE

### NEIL WHITE

ELMBRIDGE MUSEUM

SUTTON PUBLISHING LIMITED

Sutton Publishing Limited
Phoenix Mill · Thrupp · Stroud
Gloucestershire · GL5 2BU

First published 1997

Copyright © Neil White, 1997

Title page picture: players from Walton and
Hersham FC after they beat Slough FC in
April 1973.

**British Library Cataloguing in Publication Data**
A catalogue record for this book is available from the
British Library.

ISBN 0-7509-1402-5

Typeset in 10/12 Perpetua.
Typesetting and origination by
Sutton Publishing Limited.
Printed in Great Britain by
Ebenezer Baylis, Worcester.

A watercart belonging to Walton Urban District Council beside an entrance lodge to the Ashley Park
Estate, Ashley Road, Walton-on-Thames, *c.* 1910. Before the introduction of tarmac road surfaces, water
had to be sprayed on to the gravel road surface in the summer months to reduce the amount of dust
generated by passing vehicles. The Hirons family were contractors to the Walton Urban District Council.
The lettering on the cart reads, 'Walton-on-Thames Urban District Council, H. Wilde, Surveyor'.

# CONTENTS

A studio portrait of Mr William T. Hirons of Walton-on-Thames, *c.* 1900. Mr William Hirons is wearing his best three-piece suit and pocket watch; he was about thirty when this photograph was taken. The Hirons were a well-known Walton family who were builders and carters as well as contractors to Walton Urban District Council. William's father, Arthur Hirons, ran a contracting business from Fishmore Farm off Cottimore Lane, working for George Miskin and later for Walton Urban District Council again.

# INTRODUCTION

W *alton-on-Thames and Weybridge in Old Photographs* is a fascinating record of the changing faces of two very distinctive Thames-side towns, who have shared a common heritage over the years. This book has been divided into chapters which look at local families, agriculture, industry, shops and shopping, public houses, transport, local government, leisure, wartime, houses, religion, sport, the film industry and cinemas.

All the photographs used in this book come from the collections at Elmbridge Museum, located in Weybridge, Surrey. The museum was originally established in 1909 by Weybridge Urban District Council as the Weybridge Museum and was run by volunteers. In 1933 it became the museum for Walton-on-Thames and Weybridge. From 1974 it became the museum for the new Elmbridge Borough Council, covering the history of seventeen towns and villages.

Walton-on-Thames has always been an important town because of its physical location on the banks of the River Thames and good transport links with London and the south-coast towns and ports. Walton-on-Thames was known as Waltone, town of the Britons, in the Domesday survey and it is likely that there was a pre-Anglo-Saxon settlement or enclosure there. The first recorded mention of Weybridge is in AD 675 when it was recorded as Waigebrugge or Weibrugge. By the time of the Domesday survey, it was known as Weybruge and in 1294 as Weybrigge.

Transport links have been crucial to the development of both towns over the centuries. Samuel Dicker built the first bridge across the Thames at Walton in 1750 – before that, people had crossed the Thames by ferry. Walton acquired a second bridge in 1779. A third bridge was built in 1864 to replace the second one which fell down overnight in 1859, and this was later followed by a fourth in 1954. Weybridge probably had a bridge in the Anglo-Saxon period, located near the end of the present-day Bridge Street. The earliest mention of the bridge is in 1571 when a 240-foot-long wooden structure crossed the Thames. Queen Elizabeth I had to pay for the maintenance of the bridge as she was lord of the adjoining manorial lands. By 1808 the bridge had been rebuilt on thirteen wooden arches and was later replaced with a brick and iron structure in 1865. A second bridge was built from Balfour Road in 1939.

Both towns owe their current size and status to the Victorian period when they grew at an unprecedented rate after the coming of the railway in 1838. The railway brought a new business class to the area who required houses, shops and churches, and good transport links to move their manufactured goods and agricultural produce to market. People also came to live in the area to commute to London and elsewhere. Skilled artisans and labourers soon moved into the area and provided the services required by the middle classes. Later on, new trades and industries moved into the locality to service the local economy. The pre-industrial agricultural economy survived and changed to suit these new times. However, many farms and estates were swallowed up in the rapid housing development of the late nineteenth century.

The origins of local government in the area can be traced back to the Anglo-Saxon period when the area was called the Elmbridge Hundred, one of fourteen Hundreds in Surrey. The modern form of local government was established in 1895 when Walton-on-Thames and Weybridge both acquired their own urban district councils. Later, these were merged in 1933 in an effort to rationalize local administration and a new authority, Walton and Weybridge Urban District Council, was formed. This survived until 1974 when it was merged with Esher Urban District Council to form the new authority, Elmbridge Borough Council. The present-day local authority can trace itself back 1,000 years to the days of the Elmbridge Hundred.

*Walton-on-Thames and Weybridge in Old Photographs* was never intended to be an exhaustive account of the development of the two towns. Instead, it is hoped that this selection of photographs will provide a glimpse into the past lives of local people and the places where they lived, worked and enjoyed themselves. I hope that this book will help jog the memories of some older readers who may remember many of the scenes illustrated on the following pages, as well as generating an interest in all things historical among a younger generation.

I would like to thank all the staff at Elmbridge Museum who have been very supportive while I have been writing this book. Finally, a very special thank you to my wife Sheila and my son Jamie for their constant support and patience over the last few months.

*Neil White*
*Museum Manager (Elmbridge Museum)*
*August 1997*

Mary Bell with her two children, Roland and Phyllis, in 1915. The Bell family ran a clothier's shop in Church Street, Walton-on-Thames, for many years after A.C. Bell bought an outfitter's shop from 'Collier the London Clothier' in 1907. The shop remained in the family until it was closed in 1974, to make way for a new Lloyds bank.

# FAMILIES

*Mr Arthur Cobbett writing at his desk in his study at Firfield, his home in Weybridge, in the 1870s. Firfield, which was built in 1862 on Weybridge Heath, was designed by Mr Cobbett who was a successful London grocer and tea merchant. He had nine children and came to live in Weybridge because of its healthy climate and beautiful views. Mr Cobbett died in 1891 aged seventy-six.*

Mr and Mrs Warwick Deeping relaxing in the garden of their house, Eastlands, Weybridge, in the 1930s. Deeping at first planned a career in medicine and during the First World War served in the Royal Army Medical Corps (RAMC) in Gallipoli, Egypt and France. He came to live in Weybridge in 1919 and abandoned his career in medicine for writing. In 1925 his novel, *Sorrell and Son*, became a best-seller and for the next twenty-five years he wrote a series of romantic stories, some of which were later made into successful films. He developed his house by purchasing the land around it, including the next-door cottage. After his death in 1952, his wife opened the grounds to the public twice a year in aid of the District Nurses' Association.

Mr Edwards with his son on the steps of their house in Jessamy Road, Weybridge, *c.* 1920. They are both wearing the typical working dress of the period, suit trousers, waistcoats and collarless shirts. The family cat also appears in this photograph.

Paul Spriggs, aged five, wearing his school
uniform and holding a cricket bat in the family
garden. This photograph was taken near
Weybridge Heath in the 1950s.

The Victorian novelist and poet, George
Meredith, with his son Arthur in 1864. At this
time Meredith was living at Copseham
Cottage, Round Hill, near Esher Common.
Previously he had been living with the well-
known sculptor, Francis John Williamson, at
Fairholme, his house in the High Street, Esher.
From 1848 to 1853, Meredith and his wife
May lived at The Limes in the Quadrant,
Weybridge. The many woods and commons
surrounding Weybridge were a great source of
inspiration for Meredith. His first book of
verse, *The Pastorals*, was mainly written on
St George's Hill, and many other poems
including 'Robin Redbreast', and his novel,
*Richard Feveral*, were also inspired by the area.

Four generations of the Baker family of Walton-on-Thames in the 1950s. The photograph shows Mrs A. Vernon, Mrs A. Baker, Mrs Webster, who was Mrs Vernon's daughter, and Mrs Baker's granddaughter holding her new baby. The family lived at Ivy Cottage in Ashley Road, Walton-on-Thames.

# ON THE LAND

*A line drawing showing the Miskin Merchant's wood yard and Miskin Farm, located in Terrace Road, Walton-on-Thames, in about 1900. Mr George Miskin originally started his wood yard business in Walton-on-Thames and from 1921 he traded under a new name, Gridley Miskin, after the acquisition of F. Gridley's wood yard in Hampton Wick. In 1988 Gridley Miskin was purchased by the firm Harcros, who still trade from the site of the original Miskin wood yard.*

Tractors and other farm equipment in the machinery shed at Rivernook Farm, Walton-on-Thames, in 1974. This and the following photographs were all taken by the staff of Weybridge Museum (now Elmbridge Museum) on 1 August 1974.

The packaging and loading shed at Rivernook Farm, Walton-on-Thames, 1974. Inside the shed can be seen a fork-lift truck used for loading pallets of farm produce on to lorries.

Workers returning from the fields with a tractor and trailer load of cauliflowers stacked in wooden crates. The farm's greenhouses are to the right of the tractor and trailer. This tractor has special narrow tyres to enable it to drive between the rows of produce growing in the fields.

An interesting photograph showing gravel workings seen across the fields at Rivernook Farm in 1974. At this time gravel was being extracted by the local water board from neighbouring land. Once the gravel pits were exhausted, the pits would be filled in with domestic refuse from London and elsewhere.

The Hirons family of Walton-on-Thames also owned Fishmore Farm as well as doing other work in the area. This view from 1910 shows members of the Hirons family at the farm with a mare and a new-born foal.

A young girl having a pony ride on Bluebird, a horse at the Fishmore Farm riding school, Walton-on-Thames, c. 1948. The riding school was established in 1931 by Mr W. Hirons.

Mr Hirons standing with a horse at the Fishmore Farm riding school, Walton-on-Thames, in 1959. It is interesting to note that Mr Hirons is wearing the work clothes of his youth, a three-piece black suit, collarless shirt and pocket watch on a chain, plus, of course, the obligatory cloth cap. This view clearly demonstrates the flat nature of the land in this part of Walton-on-Thames.

A smartly turned out horse and trap at Fishmore Farm, Walton-on-Thames, 1910. The Hirons family were also carriers, using their own horses for all manner of local contract work. In the summer months before the First World War they were contracted by Walton Urban District Council to haul a horse-drawn water cart around the district, dampening down the surface of the gravel roads. This job became unnecessary with the introduction of tarmac road surfaces in the 1920s.

A reminder of what life was like on a farm before the introduction of tractors and other labour-saving machines. This picture shows ploughing at Fishmore Farm, Walton-on-Thames, using a team of horses, in about 1954. Throughout the 1930s and 1940s horse-drawn ploughing was fast becoming obsolete with the introduction of tractors. However, fuel restrictions during the Second World War caused a short revival in the use of horses.

Mr Hirons working with a horse at Fishmore Farm, Walton-on-Thames, in 1954.

Two land girls at Rivernook Farm, Walton-on-Thames, c. 1946. During the Second World War young women were drafted into the Women's Land Army to work the land and fill the roles left empty by men joining the forces. They effectively helped feed the country from 1940 until 1948 when the Land Army was officially abolished. At its peak over 100,000 women worked in the Land Army. They wore a standard uniform issued by the government, which consisted of khaki breeches, leather boots, jerkins, shirts and jumpers, and hats for working in the fields during the summer months. Many of them lived with the farmer's family or in special billets and all received regular salaries. For many of them it was their first taste of country life and working out of doors.

Cows grazing in a field off Cottimore Lane, Walton-on-Thames, *c*. 1900. They belonged to the Uglow family who ran a butcher's shop in 79 Terrace Road, Walton-on-Thames, where they butchered their own meat. Uglow's cattle were brought to Walton by train and unloaded in the goods yard. They were then walked through the town to their field. It was a common sight until after the Second World War to see cows being herded through Walton town centre, where they often strayed into local shops, causing much alarm.

A postcard view of Hamm Court Farm, just outside Weybridge, in the 1880s. This site was once in the possession of King Henry I. In 1481 it was given to the Dean and Canons of St George's chapel, Windsor, by Sir Thomas Seyntleger, on condition that it was used to support a chantry to pay for the cost of employing a priest to say prayers for his dead wife. Over the years it has had various owners until it was acquired in 1823 by the 4th Earl of Portmore who demolished the old building and converted the stable block into a house. Red deer were introduced to the farm from Petworth Park in 1979.

The farmhouse at Hamm Court Farm, Weybridge, 1968. This photograph was taken by museum staff when the farm was unoccupied. Mr and Mrs Bransden later moved into the premises.

Brooklands Farm, Weybridge, 1914. At this date Brooklands Farm was linked to the Brooklands estate which was owned by the Locke King family. They built the famous Brooklands racetrack in 1907. By this time the farm was empty and in a very dilapidated condition. It was demolished in the 1970s.

Mr Higgs and Miss A. Higgs of Higgs Farm, Weybridge, photographed in 1925 by Mr F. Foote. It was certainly taken in the summer months to judge by the long shadows and the light summer dress that Miss A. Higgs is wearing. Mr Higgs, however, has made no concession to the weather; he is wearing his heavy wool, three-piece suit, Homburg hat, shirt, bow-tie and heavy boots. He is also wearing his pocket watch.

Another photograph by Mr F. Foote of a horse outside the stable block at Higgs Farm, Weybridge, 1925.

Cows being driven past a row of shops at the Halfway, Walton-on-Thames, in the early 1900s. They are walking from Walton-on-Thames railway station, where they have been unloaded from cattle wagons, to Walton town centre. From there they will be sent on to local farms or to a local slaughterhouse. As mentioned earlier, some butchers, like the Uglow family, kept their own herds of cows in local fields until they needed them. Most of the traffic on the roads at this time consisted of horse-drawn vehicles, represented by the carriage waiting outside a shop on the left of the picture.

Mr Kilminster photographed at Higgs' dairy, Weybridge, c. 1935–6. Mr Kilminster is seen here with the handcart he used to deliver fresh milk from the farm to houses and businesses in the district. In those days people would receive their milk fresh from a local dairy, usually run, as in this case, by a local farm. It must have been very hard work pushing this handcart up and down the many streets in the area. The tyres on this handcart are pneumatic and this was quite unusual as most others had the old-fashioned wooden wheels with iron tyres. By this time milk was delivered in glass bottles, note the wire milk-bottle basket that Mr Kilminster is holding. Earlier in the century, milk was delivered in metal containers and ladled out according to the quantity required by the customer.

# INDUSTRY

*The boiler house at the Thames Water Authority pumping station, Walton Road, Walton-on-Thames, 1975. Nearby in Hurst Road, West Molesey, the Thames Water Authority had a pumping station with a Hathorn Davey triple-expansion engine, installed in 1911–12. This was in daily use until it was dismantled in 1975.*

A Thames barge unloading at Coxes Lock Mill, near Weybridge, in the 1950s.

Barges moored on the Thames at Whittets Oil Mill, near Thames Lock, Wey Navigation, Weybridge, 1924. This photograph was taken upstream of the Thames Lock looking towards the mill. Two narrow boats are seen lying opposite the mill and one wide barge is moored upstream. It is just possible that this photograph was taken by the master of St George's College, Addlestone.

Workmen laying electricity cables from Thames Street to the foot of Monument Hill, Weybridge, 1901–2. The works' foreman, the gentleman wearing the suit and straw boater, is looking on as two workmen pour tar on to the electricity cables at the bottom of the ditch. Two other workmen wait in the background with their bucket of hot tar. To the left of the ditch can be seen sewage pipes and insulation bricks. In the background other teams of workmen are doing similar tasks.

These works were carried out by the Urban Electricity Supply Company who built a generating station in Thames Street, Weybridge. The Weybridge village hall in Princes Road was illuminated in September 1902 and by 1911 over 800 residents were using electricity in the area. However, Weybridge had had electric lighting before. In 1890 a generating station was built in Church Walk. Local people objected so much to the new technology that the newly established Weybridge Urban District Council changed back to gas lighting in 1895.

Employees outside the Zenith Motors Ltd premises in High Street, Weybridge, in the 1920s. To the left of the building can be seen the façade of Vernon House. This photograph was clearly taken in the winter months as all the men are wearing heavy overcoats and cloth caps, except for two who are bare-headed and one who wears a soft hat. A small boy is visible in the front row.

Laundry staff at work in the Weybridge and District Laundry, *c.* 1910. Before the invention of the electric domestic washing machine in the 1950s, many people sent their washing to a laundry such as this one. Doing the washing at home was a lengthy and time-consuming business and was often performed by a washerwoman in the larger houses of the district.

Mr William Duke at work in Weybridge in the 1920s. Mr Duke was a member of the Amalgamated Society of Carpenters and Joiners and Elmbridge museum has his union cards for the years 1918, 1922, 1929 and 1932. During the First World War Mr Duke served in the Merchant Navy and in the British Army. Like most other men of his generation, he is wearing heavy trousers, a waistcoat, white shirt and hat, as well as his carpenter's apron. He also appears to be smoking a pipe while he works.

Mr George Miskin, founder of the Miskin timber business that had premises in Terrace Road, Walton-on-Thames, photographed in about 1920.

A lady standing in the porch of a house built in Walton-on-Thames by William Hirons. This photograph dates from about 1910. This was the same Hirons family who owned Fishmore Farm.

Bakery staff in Walton-on-Thames at an unidentified location, *c*. 1890. The nineteen men and one dog seem to be standing outside a domestic residence rather than a works' premises, judging by the curved windows of the house, the trellises and the creepers climbing the walls.

Members of the Chitty family and employees standing beside a house on a building site, Walton-on-Thames, in the 1890s. The Chitty family were builders by profession. Note the man in the foreground with the wooden wheelbarrow, standing beside the pile of bricks. Many of the bricks used locally came from the brickworks in Oxshott and Claygate, where there was plentiful supplies of the right kind of earth for brick manufacture. The age range of the workmen pictured here would have been very wide; the boy apprentice was probably about fourteen while the oldest man would have been aged about sixty.

The polishing workshop in the factory owned by Claudius Ash & Sons, 9 High Street, Walton-on-Thames, *c.* 1914. In 1896, Edward Power established a factory producing dental equipment in Walton-on-Thames which was taken over by Claudius Ash & Sons in 1907, with Edward Power as director. In 1924 this became the Amalgamated Dental Factory and a large complex was built on the north side of Churchfield Road. The old factory was demolished in 1936, the same year that Edward Power died, aged eighty-one. All the equipment in this photograph was driven by leather belts powered by an overhead driveshaft, connected to a stationery steam engine. With the continuous whine of the overhead belts the work conditions were very dusty and noisy; however, it was possible to shut off individual belt drives by pulling or pushing an overhead lever. This gave rise to the expression 'knocking-off'!

The machine shop at the Amalgamated Dental Factory, Walton-on-Thames, 1967. Conditions for the workforce in this photograph have improved dramatically over the intervening forty years; by this time the factory was employing around 1,000 people. The factory was closed during the economic recession of 1981.

High-tension equipment in the electricity works, Thames Street, Weybridge, in the 1920s. This equipment was installed to supply electricity to the Weybridge district; at that time there was no national grid and supplies were generated locally.

Plumbers employed by W.G. Tarrant while building luxury houses on St George's Hill, Weybridge, c. 1912–13. In total there are seventeen boys and men with their tools of the trade; they are photographed standing beside one of the wooden cottages constructed for the servants of the prospective owners of the large houses then being built on the hill.

# SHOPS

*Three delivery vans outside Rogers & Sons' electrical shop at 51 High Street, Weybridge, in the 1950s. Rogers & Sons had been selling radios and other electrical goods in Weybridge since the 1920s and by the time this photograph was taken in the early 1950s, they were selling televisions as well. Rogers were well known nationally for the high quality of their radio sets.*

The cycle shop run by W.E. Birkhead and Son in Church Street, Walton-on-Thames, 1910. It is interesting to note that the shop was called the Church Street Cycle Depot on the sign on the right-hand side. The shop also offered a plating and enamelling service.

Lewis and Sons (Weybridge) Ltd cycle shop in The Quadrant, Weybridge, photographed in July 1981. Lewis and Sons opened a shop selling motorcycles in 1908 and for many years displayed a model 1914 Triumph and 1921 BSA in the shop window. The houses and shops in The Quadrant were built on the site of the former entrance to the Portmore Park Estate in the 1880s and 1890s, with the last row of shops to be completed in 1897.

A parade of shops in Queen's Road, Weybridge, 1925. This photograph, taken by Cecil Gould, was reproduced in the official guide to the area which was produced by Weybridge Urban District Council. On the right can be seen Bannister's millinery shop and outfitters. Queen's Road got its name from its associations with Queen Victoria, who used the road when travelling from Windsor Castle to Esher to visit her relations, the Duke and Duchess of Albany and Saxe-Coburg Gotha, who lived at Claremont House.

A much earlier photograph of Queen's Road, Weybridge, taken in 1908 by C.W. Sillence. This is reproduced from the Weybridge Urban District official guide to the area and shows an early motor car running past a parade of shops on the right. This scene was much altered after the First World War, when many of the Victorian buildings were replaced.

Frisby's boot store in Baker Street, Weybridge, 1906. The windows advertise 'Frisbenia Boot Polish' and 'Frisby's Boots'.

Howard's fish shop in Baker Street, Weybridge, in the 1890s. Mr Howard is standing outside the shop which also sold poultry. Howard's had another fish shop in Oatlands Park and also one in Church Street, Weybridge, which traded until the 1970s.

Shops at the junction of Baker Street and Church Street, Weybridge, *c.* 1890. For many years the cottage on the left of the photograph was the business premises of Newman's, who sold corn, coke and coal to the local inhabitants. It was later sold and demolished to make way for the National Westminster bank, which was opened in 1897. The building on the opposite side of the street belonged to R. Cock, who ran a stationery and printing business.

Shoppers in Sainsbury's, High Street, Weybridge, in the 1960s. Sainsbury's had a very ornate store in Weybridge with decorative wooden panelling and art noveau wall tiles. The floor was also highly decorated with a mosaic floral design. When the shop closed down, the decorative tiles were sold and many local people purchased them as souvenirs.

A. Lock and Sons' toy shop at 52 High Street, Weybridge, *c.* 1910. Mr E. Lock, the owner, is seen standing outside the front door to his first shop.

A thatched cottage in the High Street, Weybridge, *c.* 1890. This cottage was later demolished to make way for a Woolworth's store, which, in turn, has now gone from the High Street. The cottage probably dated from the eighteenth century with its typical thatched roof, lattice windows and dormer windows on the second floor.

A postcard view showing the junction of the High Street and New Zealand Avenue, Walton-on-Thames, in the 1950s. On the right is the United Dairies shop and opposite, on the other side of the road, is The Kiwi public house. This was named in memory of the town's links with New Zealand which were forged during the First World War, when Mount Felix was used as a military hospital by the New Zealand Army.

Thomas Dix's butcher's shop in Church Street, Weybridge, c. 1900. The shop canopy has an impressive array of meat carcasses hung from it, a practice now discontinued due to food hygiene regulations. Mr Dix and his assistant are seen standing proudly outside the shop.

The interior of Trimby's shop, 83 Hersham Road, Walton-on-Thames, Christmas 1993. Mrs Woods, the shop manager, is on the right with two young shop assistants. Trimby's was a draper's and haberdashery shop for nearly a hundred years until it finally closed in 1994. Originally built as a private house in the 1840s, it was converted into a shop in the 1880s. It was once a milliner's shop run by Mrs Emily Mahon until it was taken over by the Trimby sisters in 1896 who ran the shop until 1949. Thereafter, Mrs Parker managed the shop until 1960 when Mrs Woods took over. Some of the original shop fittings dating back to the 1880s are now on display in Elmbridge museum, including the original shop counter, stepladders, safe and shop till.

A view of Dolcis and other department stores viewed from the corner of Church Street, High Street and Hepworth Way, Walton-on-Thames, in the 1970s. The wholesale development of Walton town centre in the 1960s swept away many fine buildings dating back to the eighteenth century and this changed the character of shopping in the town for ever. At the time of writing, there are plans to replace the 1960s shopping development with new shops and arcades that will hopefully be more in keeping with the character of the town.

Blocks of flats being built near Hepworth Way, Walton-on-Thames, 1964. In the foreground can be seen the construction of the multi-storey car park that is part of The Centre.

A parade of shops in Hersham Road, looking towards the High Street, Walton-on-Thames, in the 1900s.

Shoppers in Hersham Road, Walton-on-Thames, *c.* 1910. A number of shops can be seen, including Prior & Sons. This was owned by George William Prior who ran a greengrocer's business from these premises. G.W. Price had a business in Horsham Road from 1899 until the 1920s.

A view of Church Street, Walton-on-Thames, *c.* 1920. The building nearest the camera is the printing works and offices of the *Surrey Herald* newspaper which is located above the shop premises of Rawlings & Walsh Ltd, printer's and stationer's. Merrick's dairy also had a shop a few doors down the street from the *Herald* offices.

A view of Church Street, Walton-on-Thames, in the 1930s, showing the drinking fountain, motor cars and buses.

Motor cars in Church Street, Walton-on-Thames, in the 1960s. This view was taken before the redevelopment of Walton town centre in the early 1960s.

A view of Church Street from the north, Walton-on-Thames, *c.* 1910.

Another view of Church Street, Walton-on-Thames, taken in about 1937.

Mr Adam Charles Bell standing outside Bell's outfitters soon after taking over the shop from 'Colliers the London Clothier', Church Street, Walton-on-Thames, 1907.

The newly built Temple Market near the junction of Queen's Road, Hanger Hill and Oatlands Drive, Weybridge, 1931. Temple Market was built by Horace Thompson of Hersham in 1930. He already owned a large tract of land opposite Hersham railway station, from where he ran a nursery business producing vegetables, salads and soft fruit. Although Temple Market was built as a single storey building, it was later enlarged with the addition of extra flats above the shops. The name originates from a joke. The low lines and green roof tiles of the original building made someone ask of Horace Thompson whether the building was a market or a temple. Apparently he laughed and decided to call his new shops 'Temple Market'.

F. Wood & Co. ran a provision and grocery shop from the High Street, Walton-on-Thames, in the 1920s. A company delivery van is parked outside the store. Above the shop is the legend, 'Established 1777'.

# PUBLIC HOUSES

*Monument Green, Weybridge, c. 1900. This photograph shows a parade of shops on the left and in the middle of the photograph is the Ship Hotel, which was originally an eighteenth-century coaching inn. The tall stone monument was erected in 1822 by the inhabitants of Weybridge as a memorial to the late Duchess of York, wife of the Duke of York, who lived at Oatlands. She died in 1820 and is buried in St James's parish churchyard, Weybridge.*

The Plough Inn at the junction of Ashley Road and the High Street, Walton-on-Thames, *c*. 1914. At this time the public house was owned and managed by Isleworth Brewery who produced ales, stouts, wines and spirits. There has been a public house on this site since at least 1778. The building shown here was rebuilt in 1928. Cecil Hepworth used the building for filming *The Race for the Farmer's Cup* in 1909. The part of the hero was played by Mr Lewin Fitzhamon who was also the film's director. The film was only 11½ minutes long.

A postcard view of the Bear Inn, Bridge Street, Walton-on-Thames, *c*. 1920. This was another Isleworth Brewery public house, which offered stabling for horses. In this view a farmer's cart full of agricultural produce has stopped on the forecourt; no doubt the driver has gone inside for some liquid refreshment!

The Angler's Hotel, Manor Road, Walton-on-Thames, *c*. 1890. This view shows a boathouse party beside the wharf. Beyond the hotel can be seen Rosewell's wooden boathouse, which was extended after 1904.

The Duke's Head, located near the junction of Bridge Street and the High Street, Walton-on-Thames, 1950s. This famous Walton public house dated from the 1790s and survived until 1966 when it was closed down. It was finally demolished in 1970 to make way for Woolworth's; a new Duke's Head was later built in Hepworth Way.

An earlier view of the Duke's Head photographed in about 1878. When this view was taken it was known as the Duke's Head Hotel.

Another view of the Bear Inn in Bridge Street, Walton-on-Thames, c. 1890–1900. A group stand beside the building for their photograph to be taken.

The Ashley Park Hotel, Station Avenue, Walton-on-Thames, *c.* 1914. The Ashley Park Hotel was established in 1891 and was used by travellers from Walton station requiring refreshment and accommodation. The land on which the hotel stands was purchased from the Ashley Park estate in 1890, owned by Sassoon Joseph Sassoon (1855–1918).

The Ship Hotel, High Street, Weybridge, photographed on a fine summer's day in the 1930s. There are three sports cars and two saloon cars in the forecourt.

A postcard view of the Grotto Inn, Monument Hill, Weybridge, *c.* 1910. This public house was owned by Hodgson's Brewery in Kingston-upon-Thames, who had a large number of public houses in south-west London and the north Surrey area at the turn of the century.

The tap room in the Swan Hotel, Manor Road, Walton-on-Thames, 1923. The photograph shows Mr and Mrs Bale with their daughter, Louisa, standing beside her father. A stone flagon of R. White's ginger beer stands on the bar.

# TRANSPORT

*The bridge over the River Wey, Weybridge, c. 1920. The name Waigebrugge is first mentioned in AD 675 and by 1294 the village was known as Weybrigge. It is likely that a bridge has crossed the Wey since Anglo-Saxon times, near the present-day Bridge Street. In 1571 the bridge consisted of a wooden structure 240 feet long and 5¼ feet wide and it was rebuilt on thirteen wooden arches in 1808. The Victorian bridge pictured here was opened on 31 July 1865. In 1939 work was begun on a new bridge, crossing the River Wey from Balfour Road.*

Moore's garage in Baker Street, Weybridge, in the 1930s.

An ex-London South-Western Railway freight locomotive, no. 30719, hauling a mixed pick-up goods train at Weybridge station in June 1959. From the mid-1960s most local railway stations lost their goods traffic to the roads as freight yards were closed.

Filling up at Shank's Garage in Baker Street, Weybridge, *c.* 1910–20. The petrol pump has 'Pratt's Perfection Spirit' written on it.

An express passenger train passing Weybridge station, May 1959. This is the famous Merchant Navy express train on the Down Coast Express hauled by a Southern Railway streamlined Pacific class locomotive – this was designed by O.V. Bulleid. These steam locomotives were still hauling express trains on British Railways until 1967.

A horse-drawn landau-type carriage in the road beside the cricket common, Weybridge, *c.* 1900.

A pleasure steamer passing underneath Walton Bridge, *c.* 1920. This is the third Walton bridge which was opened in 1864 and built of brick, stone and iron. The first Walton bridge was opened in 1750 and consisted of a large single wooden span. It was replaced by the second Walton bridge in 1779, until it fell down in 1859. The third Walton bridge suffered bomb damage during the Second World War and was itself replaced with a temporary Bailey bridge in 1953/4.

The third and fourth Walton bridges side by side in 1974.

Construction workers building the fourth Walton bridge in the winter of 1953–4.

A print by Robert Wilkinson of London of the first Walton bridge. This was built by Samuel Dicker in 1750.

The taxi rank at Walton railway station, Station Avenue, Walton-on-Thames, c. 1912. At this time horse-drawn and petrol-driven taxis were vying for business – one of the largest operators of horse-drawn taxis was Mr Seaby. Walton Urban District Council received a petition as early as 1908 for motorized taxi-cabs to operate from the railway station into Walton-on-Thames.

Mr John James Seaby in the early 1900s. Mr Seaby operated a taxi business from Walton-on-Thames railway station in the 1900s. In her memories of this period, Mrs Joy Trevor has written of the horse-drawn taxi-cabs at Walton Railway station: 'Another early memory is the horsebus that stood by the station and the row of cabs and the cabbies with their long whips and tired-looking horses. I remember well Mr Deamand who drove his cab for my Grandfather and Mother, Charles and Jessy Sanger.'

Mr Smith driving a motor car belonging to Denham's Garage, Baker Street, Weybridge, *c.* 1910. The car has 'Denham's Garage' written on its side.

A charabanc works' outing outside the boot repairing depot in the High Street, Walton-on-Thames, *c.* 1919.

A motor cyclist with his machine in Monument Green, Weybridge, *c.* 1910.

Mr Harold Purcell and two friends riding a motor cycle-sidecar combination, Thames Street, Weybridge, c. 1925–30.

Racing car at Brooklands race track, Brooklands, Weybridge, c. 1938–9. Brooklands race track was built in 1906–7 by Hugh Locke King as the first ever purpose-built race track in Great Britain. It was unique in that it had a concrete race track which was heavily banked enabling early racing cars to attain high speeds without braking at the corners. The track soon achieved international status and in the interwar years many speed records were made and broken at the circuit. The racing track was closed in 1939 after the outbreak of war and was never reopened after 1945. Aircraft were first flown from Brooklands in 1908 and Vickers Armstrong built aircraft there during the First World War. During the Second World War two Wellington bombers were built at the Vickers factory at Brooklands. Aircraft manufacturing survived there until 1988 when British Aerospace closed the plant.

A lone motor car in The Quadrant, Weybridge, 1923. The shopping parade on the left was built in 1897, the year of Queen Victoria's Diamond Jubilee. The spire of St James' parish church can be seen towering above the premises of Luxford's, the well known Weybridge removals firm, which was established in 1860.

# PUBLIC SERVICE

*Members of the Walton-on-Thames volunteer fire brigade outside their fire station in the High Street, Walton-on-Thames, c. 1900. From 1876 the fire brigade was allowed to use the old lock-up in the High Street to store their equipment. This was later demolished and a new fire station built in its place, as seen in this photograph. From 1895 the fire service was run and administered by Walton-on-Thames Urban District Council. The fire engine was hand-operated until the service acquired its first horse-drawn, steam-powered pump in 1906. The first petrol-driven fire engine arrived in 1920.*

A view of the convalescent home, Walton-on-Thames, as depicted on a postcard mailed from Weybridge on 2 September 1906. The convalescent home was built on land given by the 1st Earl of Ellesmere for the convalescence of poor patients from London hospitals. It was opened in 1854 and could accommodate up to 300 people. In the 1860s, two new wings were added. However, by the Second World War, the hospital had gone into decline and it was finally closed by the National Health Service in 1989. At the time of writing it is being converted into private houses.

An interior view of the sorting room in the original Weybridge post office located in Heath Road, Weybridge, c. 1900. This small post office was replaced by a modern building opened in the High Street, Weybridge, in 1914.

An exterior view of the Weybridge post office in Heath Road, Weybridge, *c*. 1900.

Firemen from the Weybridge fire brigade on their Merryweather motorized fire engine, *c*. 1915. The brigade was founded in 1875 by Mr J.W. Young, a local builder, and moved into a fire station in Balfour Road, Weybridge. At that time all the firemen were volunteers, although from 1895 all their equipment was purchased out of the rates by Weybridge Urban District Council. A new horse-drawn Merryweather steam engine was purchased in 1902, followed by a petrol-driven fire engine in 1914. In 1941 all the brigades were merged to form the National Fire Service. In 1947 Surrey County Council assumed overall control of all the Surrey-wide fire brigades.

A telegraph boy from Weybridge post office sitting on his bicycle, c. 1930. He is wearing a standard uniform issued to all post office telegraph boys at that time. He was about fourteen years old when this photograph was taken.

Council workmen with a Weybridge Urban District Council refuse cart decorated for May Day, c. 1905.

Walton library, High Street, c. 1920. Walton library was opened by Surrey County Council in 1930 and located in the Elmgrove offices. In 1932 it was moved to the building formerly used by Walton Infants' School.

Walton post office, Halfway, Walton-on-Thames, c. 1930. The fact that this building resembles a private house more than a post office was probably a deliberate decision. It was opened in 1908 and still operates as the post office today.

Walton town hall nearing completion in 1965–6. Walton and Weybridge Urban District Council built a new town hall next to The Centre as its contribution to the development of the town centre. The new town hall was opened by Her Royal Highness Princess Margaret on 19 October 1966. It lasted until 1991 when Elmbridge Borough Council replaced it with a new Civic Centre in Esher. The building was later demolished and the site sold for redevelopment. A Sainsbury's Homebase store has now been built on the site.

The almshouses on the corner of West Grove, Walton-on-Thames, c. 1890–1900. The caption accompanying this photograph in the Walton-on-Thames official guide of 1920–1 says: 'The Almshouses Trust owns nine excellent modern cottages and a caretaker's lodge, which have in later years replaced older and inferior buildings.' The almshouses were later rebuilt into blocks of flats called Mayfield.

# LEISURE

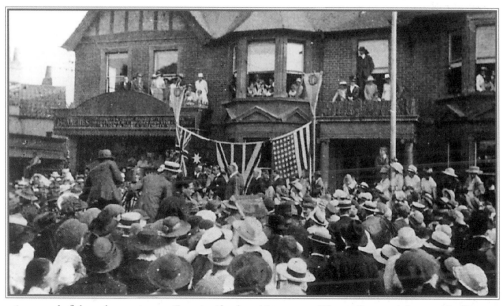

*A postcard of the welcome given to Captain Alcock and Lieutenant Whitten Brown at the council offices in the High Street, Weybridge, after their historic flight of 1919. This was the first non-stop flight across the Atlantic in a Vickers-Vimy biplane which left Newfoundland at 5.13 a.m. on 14 June and crash-landed at Clifden, County Galway, Ireland, at 9.40 a.m. on 15 June 1919. The aircraft was built by Vickers of Weybridge. Alcock and Brown both lived in the area and received a hero's welcome on their return to Weybridge. They also won the £10,000 prize given by the Daily Mail to the first aviators to fly across the Atlantic Ocean.*

A brass band standing outside G. Turner and Son, High Street, Walton-on-Thames, *c.* 1910. The brass band is probably from Hersham.

Youngsters dancing the night away at The Walton Hop in the 1960s. The Walton Hop was the first discotheque in the area and started at The Playhouse, Walton-on-Thames, by Deniz Corday in June 1958. Many famous bands played at The Hop including The Bay City Rollers, Sham 69 and The Moody Blues. Billy Fury also appeared at The Hop nearly causing a riot among his teenage female fans. Mike Read and Jonathan King started their DJ careers at The Walton Hop. The Hop survived until 1990 when it closed, after running for thirty-two years. The name is derived from the song 'At the Hop' by Danny and the Juniors which was played at the beginning and end of every Hop by Deniz Corday.

Fairground rides in Ashley Park, Walton-on-Thames, August 1901. This fair was part of the celebrations to mark the coronation of King Edward VII.

People watching television outside Rogers' shop window, the High Street, Weybridge, in the 1950s.

A postcard of Weybridge Heath, Heath Road, c. 1910. In 1909 the Weybridge Common Preservation Society was formed to prevent Weybridge Heath being redeveloped for allotments and residential housing. As a result the Heath area still gives enjoyment to many people today.

A concert by a brass band at the Churchfields Recreation Ground, Churchfields Road, Weybridge, 1966. This is a view looking across to the tennis courts and bowling green. It was taken by the first professional curator of Weybridge (now Elmbridge) museum, Mr Brian Blake.

A water colour of Baker Street, Weybridge, painted in 1882 by Miss Ada Curry. The buildings on the right-hand side of the road were once used as a theatre from about 1750 until 1800. This was pulled down in about 1901–2.

A photograph of the junction of Baker Street and the High Street, Weybridge, *c*. 1910–11. The street decorations may be for the coronation of King George V. The building on the right is the offices of Weybridge Urban District Council.

The Desborough Players' production of *Old Time Music Hall* at the Playhouse, Walton-on-Thames, in 1953. Miss Amy Gentry, who is standing on the left of the gentleman, was the founding member of the Weybridge Ladies Amateur Rowing Club in 1926.

Employees of the Walton and Weybridge Gas Company photographed before they went on a works' outing to Southend-on-Sea, travelling with the Green Luxury Coaches Company, in 1932. Behind the men can be seen the buildings of the gas works in Manor Road, Walton-on-Thames.

Camping in a skiff on the banks of the River Thames in 1913, in the style of Jerome K. Jerome's *Three Men in a Boat*. Two of the men in the boat are the brothers of Miss Ward of Walton-on-Thames who gave this photograph to Elmbridge museum; the other man is a friend.

This photograph shows the Purdue family among the crowds at a fair, possibly held in Ashley Park, Walton-on-Thames, in 1911. Mr Thomas Purdue is the gentleman standing in the front row near the rope barrier, wearing a straw boater hat, bow-tie and black suit. Behind him, to the right, is his wife, wearing a large straw hat with a ribbon, while their daughter, Winnie, is standing in front of the rope barrier wearing a white pinafore dress and straw hat. In the background can be seen steam-operated rides, including a roundabout. Also visible in the background are the showmen's booths and their travelling wooden caravans. The little boy in the immediate foreground appears to be taking part in an egg-and-spoon race.

The 1st Walton St Mary's guides and brownies pack, Walton-on-Thames, 1922. Mrs Muriel Mason, who was in the pack in 1922, gave this photograph to Elmbridge Museum.

A view of Ashley Park, Walton-on-Thames, *c.* 1910. Walton and Weybridge both had wide expanses of heath and parkland at the turn of the century. The Sassoon family owned the Ashley Park estate.

A view looking towards D'Oyly Carte Island, showing the Shepperton Ferry at Weybridge, 1915.

Phillipsons' library, Bridge Street, Walton-on-Thames, *c.* 1912. Phillipsons' was a bookbinder's as well as a lending library. Further along the road is a paperhanger's and a brewery called Brandons. Phillipsons' had another library in nearby Kingston-upon-Thames.

A postcard of the High Street, Weybridge, showing the Holstein Hall. The hall dates from 1906 and was once part of Holstein House. Mendelssohn's *Elijah* was performed there by the Weybridge Choral Society in 1906. The hall fell into decline and was later used as an early cinema, leased for industrial use and finally demolished in the early 1960s.

# EDUCATION

*A class of girls at St James's School, Baker Street, Weybridge, c. 1907. The class consists of twenty-nine girls, all aged about eight years of age.*

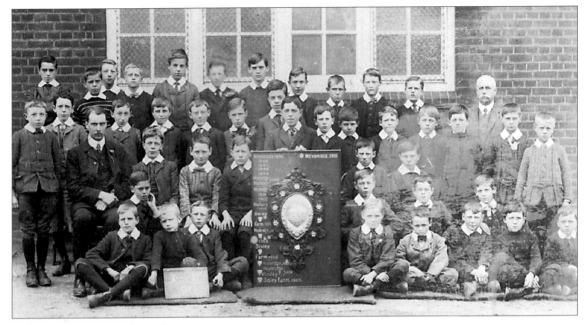

A class of boys at St James's School, Baker Street, Weybridge, *c.* 1911.

Children in the production of *Honey Pots* at St James's School, Baker Street, Weybridge, July 1930.

A class at Walton Infants' School, High Street, Walton-on-Thames, 1909. Walton Infants' School was built in 1884 on land formerly used to house the National School that opened in 1827. The infants' school moved to Ambleside Avenue in 1931 and the school was converted into a labour exchange. In 1933 it became Walton library and has remained so to this day.

Children from the Hall School, rehearsing at Bedales, Weybridge, 1929.

Inside a classroom known as the 'Glass Room' at Heath House School, Weybridge. This picture is taken from the school prospectus of 1933.

Pupils at the Hall School, Weybridge, during a lesson in the 1920s.

Pupils and teachers at Walton Infants' School (now Walton Library), High Street, Walton-on-Thames, c. 1870–80. This was probably the old Walton Infants' school prior to the building of the new school in 1881.

Boys in a production of *The Wooden Soldiers* at St James's School, Baker Street, Weybridge, in July 1930.

A woodwork class at St James's School, Baker Street, Weybridge, c. 1911–12.

A postcard view of the new Technical Institute, Weybridge, soon after it opened in November 1912. Hilda Vaughan remembers the Technical Institute's classes for girls: 'For domestic science by which we used to have to walk down to Weybridge Technical, and we had three courses down there, one course was laundry, the next one was cooking and the next one was housewifery. We learn to clean fenders, for great big stoves, and scrub tables and for the laundry we used to be able to take something every week and wash and iron. We got down there about 9 o'clock and got home by 12 o'clock, I think.'

# WARTIME

*Anti-gas drill by members of the 79 Battery, LAA, RA, Gunners, Walton-on-Thames, at Kempton Waterworks, August–September 1939. The battery was raised in the Walton area in 1938–9 and was equipped with Bofors anti-aircraft guns to help defend airfields and other military installations. The battery helped defend aircraft factories against the German airforce during the Battle of Britain in 1940. Later it was sent out to the Far East to defend the island of East Timor against Japanese invasion. Many of the battery members were captured by the Japanese and spent the war in prison camps.*

A reunion dinner at the Ashley Park Hotel, Station Avenue, Walton-on-Thames for the eighteen surviving members of the 79 Battery, LAA, RA, in 1992.

Members of the Walton-on-Thames 79 Battery, LAA, RA, preparing a gun site at Kempton Water Works, August–September 1939. Mr Birkenhead is third from the left by the gun sight.

A painting of the Flower class corvette, K-75, HMS *Celandine*, which was adopted by Walton and Weybridge Urban District Council after Warship Week in February 1942: the area raised over £500,000 for the Royal Navy. She was built in 1940 and saw action in the North Atlantic, helping to protect convoys from German submarine attack. She helped sink *U-556* off Cape Farewell, Iceland, on 27 June 1941. She was finally scrapped in Northern Ireland in 1948.

A photograph of HMS *Celandine*'s captain, Lieutenant Commander P.V. Collings (nearest the camera), on the bridge with Lieutenant Arnold, *c*. 1942–4. Lieutenant Arnold was involved in the rescue of the crew of a torpedoed Canadian destroyer, *Ottawa*, in 1942.

Members of the no. 244 Motorized Transport Corps, Army Service Corps, in training in Holcombe, Somerset, before going off to the Front in 1915. This unit was raised locally in Weybridge and Addlestone by Major Gordon Watney, who had an engineering works in the area. The unit was known affectionately as 'The Watney Lads' and eventually served in the Balkans from 1916–19. The unit provided transport for the British Army fighting there.

Peace celebrations in the High Street, Walton-on-Thames, in the summer of 1919. These were held to celebrate the end of the First World War on 11 November 1918.

Twenty-one years later Britain was again at war with Germany. This photograph shows the burial of unidentified air raid victims in Burvale Cemetery, Walton-on-Thames. They were killed when the German air force bombed the Vickers-Armstrong aircraft factory in Weybridge on 4 September 1940. This attack killed 83 people and injured 176.

Volunteers from the 6th Platoon of the Weybridge Home Guard clearing up the wreckage at the Electric Furnace Company premises in Queen's Road, Weybridge, after an air raid in 1944–5.

Auxiliary fire service personnel outside Elmgrove, Walton-on-Thames, with a hand-drawn water pump, 1938. Every urban district council had to make civil defence provisions in the lead-up to the outbreak of the Second World War. Mr Moth is standing third from the left.

A patriotic clown troupe, part of the Grand Patriotic Procession held in Weybridge on 28 June 1900 to celebrate British victories in the South African Boer War (1899–1902).

The Walton war memorial at the junction of New Zealand Avenue, High Street, Hersham Road and Ashley Road. It is seen here in the 1930s. This memorial was unveiled on 10 July 1921 before an audience of 3,000 people.

The unveiling of the Weybridge war memorial by Earl Beatty on 18 March 1923.

A photograph of Mr Robert Searle of Walton-on-Thames in the uniform of the East Surrey Regiment, 1914.

A view of Mount Felix, Bridge Street, Walton-on-Thames, *c*. 1915–19. Mount Felix was a large palatial mansion overlooking the River Thames beside Walton Bridge. During the First World War it was used by the New Zealand Army as a military hospital from 1915 until 1919. In the four years it was operating it treated 23,000 patients.

A postcard of King George V and Queen Mary visiting Mount Felix Military Hospital in 1917. The caption on the postcard reads: 'Their Majesties The King and Queen, and His R.H. The Prince of Wales at The New Zealand Military Hospital, Walton-on-Thames.'

Mount Felix Military Hospital at Christmas 1916. This shows a Christmas party for the wounded soldiers in one of the wards. This particular ward was in a hut specially constructed on land beside Oatlands Drive, opposite the mansion.

A Victory in Europe (VE) Day party held in Florence Road, Walton-on-Thames, May 1945.

A queue outside A. Lock's greengrocer's, High Street, Weybridge, 1914. This was the first Weybridge potato queue of the First World War.

A shop decorated with patriotic messages in celebration of the Relief of Mafeking during the South African Boer War, High Street, Weybridge, 1901.

Shops, including the old Weybridge Theatre, decorated to celebrate the Relief of Mafeking in the South African Boer War in 1901.

A First World War view of Baker Street, Weybridge, showing sailors and soldiers, c. 1914–18.

# THE BIG HOUSE

*Ashley House seen from the front in 1921. Ashley House was a Jacobean house built between 1602 and 1607 by Lady Jane Berkeley. Subsequent owners of the house included the 1st Earl of Anglesey, Christopher Villiers, Benjamin Weston, Richard Boyle and Viscount Shannon (who has a large memorial in St Mary's Church, Walton-on-Thames). In 1786 Sir Henry Fletcher acquired the property. It remained in the family until it was sold to David Sassoon in the 1860s. When the last male Sassoon died in 1922 without an heir, the estate was broken up for housing development and the house was demolished. An American bought the fine late seventeenth-century staircase and panelling from some of the rooms. New Zealand Avenue was constructed across the estate in 1935 by Walton and Weybridge Urban District Council.*

A flock of geese beside the barn at Ashley Park Estate in 1921.

The main staircase in Ashley House, Walton-on-Thames, 1923. This was later sold to an American after the sale of the house and estate in the same year.

The panelled hall in Ashley House, Walton-on-Thames, in 1923.

Another view of the farm on the estate; this view shows haymaking at Ashley Park in 1921.

The Old Manor House, Walton-on-Thames, *c.* 1900. This is the oldest building in Walton and dates back to the 1400s when it was once part of the Manor of Walton Leigh. During the nineteenth century the house was let to tenants and became very dilapidated. It was saved from destruction by Mr Lowther Bridger who bought it before the First World War. It was restored in the 1950s and is now a private house.

In the 1870s cottages were built in front of the Manor House, obscuring its view of the River Thames. This photograph shows the cottages in 1961.

A side view of the Manor House, Manor Road, Walton-on-Thames, in the early 1900s.

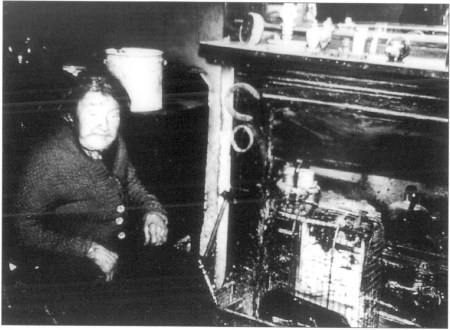

Miss Smith was an elderly tenant living in one of the cottages in Manor Road, Walton-on-Thames. This photograph shows her seated by the kitchen range in 1971, shortly before she was evicted from the cottages by Walton and Weybridge Urban District Council Environmental Health Department. All the cottages were declared unfit for human habitation and subsequently demolished, thereby opening up a vista through to the medieval Manor House.

The entrance gates to Mount Felix, Bridge Street, Walton-on-Thames, 1921.

A view of Mount Felix while it was being used as a military hospital by the New Zealand Army during the First World War. This photograph shows the sheer size of the building, which dominated the skyline of Walton-on-Thames for many years. The house was originally a Georgian mansion which was substantially rebuilt in the 1840s by the Tankerville family in the fashionable Italianate style.

Sadly this photograph shows the almost
complete demolition of Mount Felix in 1968.
By the 1960s the house was lived in by tenants
and was in a very poor condition. In 1965 the
house was purchased by Walton and
Weybridge Urban District Council for
£60,000. In 1966 a fire broke out in the roof
and a decision was taken by the council to
demolish the building and sell the land for
redevelopment. By 1968, as this photograph
shows, the house had all but disappeared. The
Council later sold the land for £400,000 to a
developer who built elegant flats on the site.

A skyline view of Mount Felix as seen from the new multi-storey car park in Hepworth Way, Walton-on-
Thames, 1965.

Swiss Cottage, which once stood on the corner of Queen's Road and Oatlands Avenue, Weybridge, *c.* 1920. The house was subsequently demolished by Lex Motor Company – previously called Weybridge Automobiles Ltd.

The front elevation of Burcote, located in Ellesmere Road, St George's Hill, Weybridge, in the 1930s. In 1937 the Charleton family lived in the house with their two sons, Edward and John. Two lodgers, Violet White and Lilian Jones, also lived with them.

An interior view of the lounge of Burcote showing a chintz-covered settee, armchairs, footstools and other period furniture in 1934. The house was built before 1896.

The Limes, located off the Quadrant, Weybridge, c. 1900. This house was once the property of Mrs Maceroni, widow of Colonel Francis Maceroni, once aide-de-camp to the King of Naples. Mrs Maceroni took in many paying lodgers including the novelist and poet George Meredith who lived there with his wife during the first years of their marriage. The house was demolished in 1909.

Mr Gessing, coachman to the Gill family, c. 1871. Interestingly, two photographs have been pasted together to form this image. The trees in the background come from a different photograph to the original one of Mr Gessing standing beside a brick plinth. The Gill family lived at Apps Court, Walton-on-Thames, from 1854 until 1897.

Servants at River House, Manor Road, Walton-on-Thames, 31 July 1909. They are, left to right: Mr Percy Huckins, Mr William Andress, Mr George Lock, Miss B. Fenn, Miss A. Tickner and Miss M. Wady. River House was once the home of Sir Arthur Sullivan of Gilbert and Sullivan fame.

Another picture of servants, taken at River House, Manor Road, Walton-on-Thames, on 13 June 1913. Mr Percy Huckins is seated in the centre of the photograph.

River House, Manor Road, Walton-on-Thames, 1923. This property was later acquired by Walton Urban District Council.

Apps Court house and flower garden, Walton-on-Thames, December 1886.

# AT PRAYER

*St Mary's Church, Church Walk, Walton-on-Thames, c. 1900. The 1086 Domesday survey mentions a church in Walton-on-Thames, although it was almost certainly a wooden building. Much of the present church dates from the medieval period; the north arcade was added in the 1100s, the chancel in the 1300s and the south arcade in the 1400s. Some of the church bells are very old with one bell, a fifth cast by Richard Eldridge, dating from 1606.*

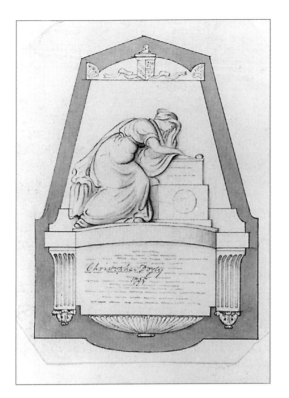

A water colour by Edward Hassell of a memorial to Christopher Doyly in St Mary's Church, dating from 1795. This picture was painted between 1823 and 1827.

A sepia view of St James's Church, Church Street, Weybridge, in about 1900. This view is taken from the fields behind the church. The area is now used as a public car park as well as housing the public library and Elmbridge museum. St James is the parish church for Weybridge. The Domesday survey did not mention a church in Weybridge, although a chapel was built much later which was attached firstly to Chertsey Abbey and later to Newark Priory. St James replaced an earlier church called St Nicholas in 1848. The present church was designed by J.L. Pearson and built in the fashionable Gothic style. Many monuments were transferred from St Nicholas to the new building, including three skeleton brasses dating from the 1400s. Other brasses transferred to the new building included ones to John Woulde (1598), Thomas Inwood (1586) and Sir John Trevor (1605).

An interior view of St James's Church in about 1950.

New bells awaiting erection in the belfry of St James's Church in 1875.

The Revd Harry Millican reading in his sitting room at Weinberg, his house in King's Road, Walton-on-Thames, *c.* 1915–20.

The Revd Baron's Sunday school teachers, Weybridge, *c.* 1880. The Revd Baron was minister of the Congregational church which was located in Queen's Road from 1865 until 1890.

The Catholic church, Walton-on-Thames, *c.* 1920.

The Congregational Church in Queen's Road, Weybridge, *c.* 1925.

The Wesleyan Church, Heath Road, Weybridge, in 1909.

A postcard view of the St Charles Borromeo Roman Catholic church, Heath Road, Weybridge, *c.* 1910. James Taylor built a small Roman Catholic chapel in the grounds of his house in 1835, which was used for his own family's needs. In February 1848 the French King Louis Phillipe abdicated and took up residence at Claremont near Esher. However, Claremont was crown property and not suitable for Catholic worship. The exiled French king and his queen attended their first Roman Catholic mass at James Taylor's small chapel on 7 March 1848. This started a connection with the royal family of Orléans, which saw thirteen of its members buried in the vault underneath the chapel. Later, the bodies were removed to Dreux in France, where other members of the Orléans family were buried. In 1988 an application was made for the church to be demolished and replaced by flats, with the congregation moving to a new church in Minorca Fields. Happily the church was not demolished and today it is used by the North Korean community.

Another coloured postcard view of the St Charles Borromeo Catholic church in Heath Road, this time looking towards Weybridge, *c.* 1910.

A fine view of the tower of St Mary's Church, Walton-on-Thames, 1950s.

# SPORTING LIVES

*Members of Walton Swimming Club photographed outside their swimming pavilion during the Walton town regatta, 1920. The club was founded in 1912 by the Faithful brothers.*

St James's School football team, Baker Street, Weybridge, 1914. This shows the school football team and the school staff standing with a shield which lists the names of all the winning school teams from 1895 to 1914.

A cricket match on the Cricket Common, Queen's Road, Weybridge, in the 1950s.

A photograph of members of the Coachmen v. Gardeners cricket team, Queen's Road, Weybridge, 1908. The match was played on the site of a filled-in pond on the Hanger Hill end of the Cricket Common, where it has a junction with Queen's Road. The headgear the men are wearing obviously indicates what team they played for – and their occupation. The coachmen all wear top hats while the gardeners sport a mixture of headwear, from cloth caps to straw boaters.

A game of hockey on the playing fields at Heathlands Girls' School, Queen's Road, Weybridge, c. 1910–15.

A hunt meeting outside Wallin House, Bridge Street, Walton-on-Thames, *c.* 1900. Hunts still met in the area in the early 1900s but by the time of the First World War hunting had virtually died out in the district. Increased urbanization had resulted in the loss of the rural habitat for foxes as well as the open fields which could accommodate large numbers of riders and packs of hounds.

Walton Swimming Club regatta at the Walton swimming pavilion by the towpath, Walton-on-Thames, 1923.

The tennis courts at Churchfields recreation ground, Churchfield Avenue, Weybridge, in the 1920s. The 150-foot-high spire of St James's Church can be clearly seen in the background.

Miss Pansy Irene Seaby holding the Surrey Ladies Swimming Club shield, Walton-on-Thames, 1913/14.

Mr Robert Searle standing beside the back window of his house at 58 Thames Street, Walton-on-Thames, in about 1910. He is standing beside a small table which bears the two trophies he won at billiards matches in the Walton Working Men's Club before the First World War. Mr Searle was born in 1889.

Members of the Weybridge Ladies Amateur Rowing Club at a rowing regatta in France in about 1928–9.

Miss Amy Gentry was captain and chairwoman of the Weybridge Ladies Amateur Rowing Club. Here she is photographed receiving the Women's Amateur Sculling Championship cup in 1930. Amy Gentry was the founding figure behind the establishment of the club in 1926; previously she had been rowing with the Weybridge Rowing Club which had only started to admit female members in 1920. She is wearing the very distinctive WLARC blazer.

The opening of the new Walton Swimming Club pavilion on Saturday 16 June 1934.

The Amalgamated Dental Factory bowling team with a cup, Walton-on-Thames, *c.* 1967.

# GOING TO THE MOVIES

*A portrait of Cecil Hepworth, c. 1900. Hepworth was the genius behind the founding of a film studio in Hurst Grove, Walton-on-Thames, in 1899, three years after the first public showing of a film in Great Britain. Hepworth's interest in film and photography was inherited from his father who was a renowned operator of the Victorian magic lantern. Hepworth established one of the first film studios in the country and many of his early silent films, such as* Rescued by Rover *(1905), went on to achieve international fame. However, the decline in the British film industry caused by the onset of the First World War and his failure to counter the success of the American Hollywood film industry, led to the dramatic decline and eventual closure of the Walton-on-Thames film studios in 1924. Two years later, Archibald Nettlefold, a northern industrialist, purchased the studio complex and continued to make films at Walton from 1926.*

An Edwardian postcard of Miss Alma Taylor, reproduced in the Famous Star Series by Beagle's postcards in 1927. Alma Taylor was one of the leading actresses employed by Cecil Hepworth at the Walton-on-Thames film studios in the early 1900s.

A portrait of Miss Chrissie White, another Hepworth picture player and principal actress. She is seen here in the production entitled *The Winning Smile*, made at Walton-on-Thames in about 1920. Chrissie White and Alma Taylor both started working for Cecil Hepworth while they were still young girls, and went on to achieve international fame as early silent movie film stars. Chrissie White later married Henry Edwards who had been Hepworth's principal male actor. When the Hepworth Studios went into liquidation in 1924, Chrissie and Henry Edwards established their own film company.

Richard Greene starring as Robin Hood in the popular television series made for the ATV television network at the Walton film studios from 1955 to 1959. The studios eventually closed in 1961 and the site was redeveloped as part of the new Walton town centre built in the early 1960s. A new road, appropriately named Hepworth Way, was cut across the site of the former studio complex.

A line drawing by Cecil Hepworth of his first covered studio in Walton-on-Thames, *c.* 1905. Hepworth's autobiography, *Came the Dawn*, told the exciting story of early film making in Walton-on-Thames at the turn of the century.

Filming at the Nettlefold film studios, Walton-on-Thames, in the 1940s. The cameraman on the far right is Mr Arthur Grant, who started working for Hepworth in 1922.

A birthday party for Bette Davis, the American actress, at the Nettlefold film studios, Walton-on-Thames, in the 1950s.

Many of the films produced in the Walton film studios were shown in local cinemas. This photograph shows the newly opened Regal cinema in New Zealand Avenue, Walton-on-Thames. It was opened on 26 March 1938 and was managed by Clifford Spain, who had previously been the manager of the Capitol cinema from 1927 to 1938. The Regal cinema had an auditorium holding 2,000 seats and it was the only cinema in Walton-on-Thames with a restaurant . It was taken over by the ABC chain and eventually closed in 1971.

# INDEX